VOICES OF EXPERIENCE

Practical Ideas to
Spark Up the Year

Grades K-3

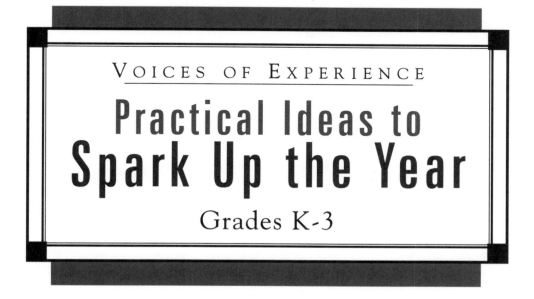

VOICES OF EXPERIENCE

Practical Ideas to
Spark Up the Year

Grades K-3

COLLEEN POLITANO • JOY PAQUIN
CAREN CAMERON • KATHLEEN GREGORY

PORTAGE & MAIN PRESS

Portage and Main Press acknowledges the financial support of the Government of Canada through the Book Publishing Industry Development Program (BPIDP) for our publishing activities.

Printed and bound in Canada by Hignell Printing

04 05 06 07 08 5 4 3 2 1

Library and Archives Canada Cataloguing in Publication

Practical ideas to spark up the year : grades K-3 / Colleen Politano ... [et al.].

(Voices of experience)
Includes bibliographical references.
ISBN 1-55379-030-8

1. Education, Primary- Activity programs. 2. Creative activities and seat work. I. Politano, Colleen, 1946- II. Series: Voices of experience (Winnipeg, Man.)

LB1537.P73 2004   372.13   C2004-904531-8

PORTAGE & MAIN PRESS

100-318 McDermot Ave.
Winnipeg, MB Canada R3A 0A2
Email: books@portageandmainpress.com
Tel: 204-987-3500
Toll-free fax: 1-866-734-8477
Toll free: 1-800-667-9673

FOR JOY PAQUIN

In the summer of 2003, the four of us (Caren, Kathleen, Joy, and Colleen) worked together and planned the ideas for all the books in the Voices of Experience series. Shortly before the first two books went to press, Joy died suddenly. The ideas in this series reflect Joy's spirit.

Joy Paquin was a teacher's teacher. She was committed to making classrooms the best places for children and to sharing ideas with others. She was known for her enthusiasm, tireless dedication, and the fun she brought to teaching. Joy did more than teach children to read and write; she taught her students and her friends  how to live a full and joyous life. Her professional legacy – one of love, caring, humor, knowledge, and wisdom – will live on for thousands of children, parents, educators, and colleagues.

We dedicate this series to Joy, our dear friend, with love.

Caren, Kathleen, and Colleen

ACKNOWLEDGMENTS

Thanks to our friends and colleagues who welcome us
into their classrooms.

Contents

Introduction

Who is this series for?

Voices of Experience is a series of six books – three for grades K-3, three for grades 4-8. Each book is full of practical ideas designed for new teachers, teachers new to a grade level, and teachers who want new ideas to reenergize their practice.

What's in the books?

We have compiled our best ideas and organized them into two sets of three books:

■ Book 1: for the start of the year when teachers are just getting to know their students

■ Book 2: for during the year when teachers need to get themselves and their students "fired up"

■ Book 3: for the end of the year when teachers need to wrap things up

Each book is organized into four sections around the acronym ROAR.

R = ideas for building **r**elationships

O = ideas for classroom **o**rganization

A = ideas for classroom **a**ssessment that support student learning

R = ideas that are **r**eliable and ready to use tomorrow

"Create a new model of teacher to teacher support so that every teacher knows every other teacher's best ideas."

— Eric Jensen,
Brain-Based Learning

For each idea we provide a brief discussion and easy-to-follow steps. Many also include student examples and unique adaptations.
In addition, we have included current information about the brain and how students learn.

We have also included a variety of ways to use this series of books to support professional development activities in different settings; for example, educators' book clubs; team and department meetings and staff meetings; in-service and pre-service workshops; and seminars with student teachers (see appendix A).

Final Note:

The single, most important message we want to leave you with is to listen to your own voice and the voices of your students. Adapt our ideas to fit for you, your students, and your school community.

INTRODUCTION TO RELATIONSHIPS

Establish trust and build relationships before anything else.
Then, place relationships above the rest.

■

Show students you care about them as people,
and let them see you as a person.

■

When relationships are established, students
can take risks and accept new challenges.

■

Emotion is a huge part of the classroom;
it often sets the stage for learning.

■

Relationships: First in the book. First in our classrooms.

In this chapter on relationships, we offer practical ideas
to "spark" things up for you and your students
during the year. Activities include ways to:

- celebrate learning

- have students teach others new skills

- make new friends in the school

- have students share their collections

- invite families into the school

Learning Parties:
taking time to celebrate

> "Modeling love of learning and creating a classroom environment where rituals and celebrations are dealt with are foundations for emotional well being."
>
> — Colleen Politano,
> Joy Paquin,
> *Brain-Based Learning*
> *With Class*

DISCUSSION

Celebrating learning throughout the year helps strengthen relationships and reenergize students. We plan "learning parties" that are not too noisy, too messy, or too much trouble by following four guidelines: involve students from the start, organize around a single learning event, follow a simple 5-step agenda, and keep the time frame short.

STEPS

1. Tell students why celebrating learning is important. For example, we say: "Taking time to celebrate learning helps everyone feel good about how hard they've worked and what they've learned. When we feel good, it helps us learn more. We are going to plan a party together to celebrate some learning we've done."

2. Decide on a specific focus for the learning party. We choose something that we have been working on in class that is manageable, such as "friendship."

3. Record an agenda for the party on a piece of chart paper, and talk about it with students (see figure 1).

4. Make a list of what is needed for the party and ask students to volunteer to bring one item (see figure 2). To avoid having too much food and to make the planning simpler, we divide the class in two groups and have only one group bring the refreshments. We reassure the second group that they will be responsible for bringing food to the next party.

Learning Party Agenda
1. set up refreshments
2. meet together for party activity
3. eat refreshments
4. clean up
5. reflection time

Figure 1. Party agenda

5. Send a note to the students' families informing them about the party (see figure 3).

6. Create a party atmosphere by having students make something that links to the learning focus. For example, for a "friendship party," have each student make a paper placemat that shows something they like to do with a friend.

7. Set guidelines with students before the party begins. We have learned not to assume that our students know basic party etiquette. We talk with students and set guidelines about behaviour. As a class, we create a "reminder list" (see figure 4).

8. Have students read over the reminders and look at the agenda one more time, just before the party starts.

9. Provide class time for a brief reflection after the party is over. For example, ask students to sit in a circle and give a brief response to an open-ended prompt such as: "I am a good friend when I ..." or "My favourite part of the party was ..."

ADAPTATION

Have parties to celebrate any part of learning, including: reading books, working together, learning new math skills, completing writing, or finishing projects.

What we need to bring

drinks	cups, plates, napkins
Natalie	WeyMing
Sultan	Palmer
Josh	John
Mercy	Andrea

main treats		sweets
Angela	Rich	Maureen
Tamara	Rasool	John V.
Railyn	Bruce	Connor
Naoto	Mark	Kellen
Wayne	Leon	Susie

Figure 2. Planning chart

Dear Families,

Our class has been learning about friendship. We will use the last hour on <u>Wednesday 15th</u> to have a party to celebrate our learning. Sharing food adds to a celebration. Your child has volunteered to bring <u>some veggies and dip for the class.</u> If this works for you please send it on the morning of the party. If not, please send something else, or let me know if we need to make other arrangements.

Thank you,
Colleen

Figure 3. Note home

Black line master on p. 55

Our Party Reminders

eat nicely

take turns to get your food

wait until everyone has food before you eat

take a few things to eat

get more food when we have second helpings

use your napkin

quietly get rid of food you don't care for

say "thanks" to people who brought stuff

talk to people around you

do your share of clean up

quiet voices

Figure 4. Party reminders

Kid-directed Centres:
giving students opportunities to show what they know

DISCUSSION

Give students opportunities to become directors of a centre where they teach peers a new skill. We find including kid-directed centres at different times of the year leads to new interests, new friendships, and new levels of confidence.

STEPS

1. Tell students there are many things they each know how to do that they could teach someone else. We offer examples to help our students understand what we mean. We say: "Erin, you know how to skateboard and you could teach other people." "Andy, I've seen you play card games that other people don't know how to play."

2. Develop a list of potential kid-directed centres with students. Ask: "Who has something they know how to make or do that they could teach someone else?" Record their ideas on chart paper (see figure 5).

3. Have one student (the director) demonstrate a kid-directed centre for the class.

Who can make or do something that they would like to teach someone else?

Candace - making pop-up pictures
Rasool - playing card games
Tamara - spool knitting
Josh - making gel pen pictures with my gel pens
Graeme - making paper airplanes
Davinder - paper weaving
Rosamund - playing checkers

Figure 5. Kid-directed centres

We help the "director" be successful by taking a few minutes before the demonstration to ask the following questions: "What are you going to teach others to do?" "What materials do you need?" "How much time do you think you will need?"

4. Meet together after the demonstration for a "how to" session to talk about possible ways to make kid-directed centres more successful. For example; how to get others to listen; how to get others to help clean up; how to get others to come to the centre.

5. Decide how often to add kid-directed centres to your regularly scheduled centre time. Post a schedule and invite volunteers to sign up. We choose one day per week to add kid-directed centres when the class needs a change, or when centres need to be sparked up.

6. Give the directors a chance to "sell" their idea at the beginning of centre time.

7. Give students a signal to indicate the end of centre time. Ask students who worked at the kid-directed centre to tell their director one thing they liked or one thing they learned.

ADAPTATION

Another type of kid-directed centre is to have students bring toys, games, and other items that they (and their families) are willing to demonstrate and share with others. Our students tend to bring items such as action figures, games, art materials, books, atlases, and favourite toys.

Figure 6. At a kid-directed centre, children follow the directions of a classmate

Trading Spaces:
making new friends

DISCUSSION

When children form friendships outside the classroom, they develop a greater sense of belonging within the school. We introduce the idea of "trading spaces" to give students an opportunity to work in different classrooms with different teachers and peers.

STEPS

1. Find one or two colleagues (preferably ones whose classrooms are close to your own) who are interested in offering an activity for students from other classrooms. Make a list of what activities each teacher will offer (see figure 7). We make sure that the activities that we offer are not too elaborate and do not create extra work for us.

> ### Choices for trading spaces
>
> | Mr. Reicken's room | Mrs. Davidson's room |
> |---|---|
> | chess (8) | science center (14) |
> | checkers(8) | math centers (14) |
> | computers (8) | |
>
> | Ms. Silverthorn's room | Mrs. Politano's room |
> |---|---|
> | train sets (6) | sewing (6) |
> | blocks (6) | flannel board (6) |
> | Lego (6) | white boards (6) |
> | Googoplex (6) | paint easels (8) |

Figure 7. Activity list

2. Select a day and time for "trading spaces." We choose two or three times during the year when things need to be "sparked up."

3. Make and post a sign-up chart for each classroom that shows the activities and the total number of students who can select each

activity. Give students an opportunity to sign up for one activity that interests them. If spaces are filled, students need to select a different activity.

4. Ask students to go to the room they chose and spend approximately 40 minutes working on the activity.

5. Have students clean up before they leave the classroom, just as a guest at someone else's house would be expected to clean up before they leave.

6. Have students return to their own classrooms to discuss their experiences "trading spaces." We pose the following questions to encourage discussion:

What did you do?

What did you like best?

What suggestions do you have for another time?

What would you like to go back and do again?

Who did you get to work with this time that you don't usually get to work with?

Who do you want to work with next time?

Where do you want to go next time?

Collections:
finding out about each other

DISCUSSION

Helping students find out about one another during the year builds new relationships. We invite students to bring collections from home to show and talk about in class. Our students are curious about each other's interests and pay close attention as peers present their collections.

STEPS

1. Bring in a collection of your own to show and talk about with students.

2. Ask students: "What collections do you already have that you might be able to bring to school?" Make a list of their responses (see figure 8). We also encourage students to think of collections they might like to start, and we add these to the list.

3. Make and post a sign-up sheet and invite anyone who is interested in sharing a collection to sign up. If all our students volunteer to bring collections, we schedule two or three students to present each day over a two- or three-week period.

> **What collections could we bring?**
>
> | | |
> |---|---|
> | sports cards | cars |
> | action figures | shoes |
> | rocks | jewelry |
> | stamps | postcards |
> | bottle caps | leaves |
> | gum wrappers | books |
> | pens | dolls |
> | coins | teddy bears |

Figure 8. Collections

4. Send a letter to families that explains when and how children will show their collections. We include sentence starters (see figure 9).

5. Give each student time to present his or her collection to the class.

6. Ask students to tell each collector one thing they learned, one thing they liked, one thing that surprised them, or one personal connection.

7. Set aside a space for students to display their collections. We designate a space and section it off with tape or string to emphasize that collections are to be looked at, not touched.

ADAPTATION

We read Marthe Jocelyn's book, *Hannah's Collections* to the class as a way to help extend the idea of collecting.

Dear Families,

Your child ___Eric___ has volunteered to bring his/her collection of ___cars___ to present to the class on ___February 2nd___.
To help everyone be successful we suggest children follow these sentence starters for their presentations:

My collection is...

Three things I want you to notice are...

One thing that might surprise you is...

Please ask me some questions about my collection of...

There will be a space set aside in the classroom for collections to be displayed.

Thank you,
Colleen

P.S. Please do not send anything that is "too precious to lose."

Figure 9. Letter about collections

Black line master on p. 56

Family Connections:
inviting families and friends to class

"When students work hard…they are anxious to have friends and family view their efforts and help celebrate their work."

— Martha Kaufeldt,
Begin With the Brain

DISCUSSION

Involve families and friends in a variety of everyday school activities to bring positive energy into the classroom. We offer three of our favourite manageable, nonthreatening ideas to make "family connections."

IDEA # 1 COME AND READ

STEPS

1. Let students know that you are going to invite family members and friends to come into the classroom to read to them.

2. Help students prepare for their guest readers by asking them to respond to the question: "What's important when we listen to guests read to us?" Record responses on chart paper (see figure 10).

3. Establish a time for guests to come and read to the class. Send invitations

What's important when we listen to guests read to us?

- look at them
- be quiet
- sit still
- keep your hands and feet to yourself
- don't interrupt
- make connections in your brain
- say thank you
- tell what we liked
- give them compliments
- ask questions after
- think about the book

Figure 10. Student responses to prepare for guest readers

that include a response slip (see figure 11). We invite guests to come at the beginning or at the end of the day over a one-week period.

4. Introduce the guest reader(s). If more than one guest has signed up on one day, organize the students into the necessary number of groups. We have guests read to students for approximately 7-10 minutes.

5. Set aside time for students to thank the guest reader(s) and offer specific compliments. We establish a tradition of playing good-bye music at the end of the "come and read" session, such as "Happy Trails to You."

Dear Families and Friends,

You are invited to come and read in our class from 9:00 - 9:15 any day in the week of January 10 -15th.

Please drop in, bring a book or feel free to use a book from our classroom library.

Thank you,
Colleen

Figure 11. "Come and Read" invitation to readers

IDEA #2 COME TO LUNCH

STEPS

1. Tell students that you are going to invite family members to come and have lunch with them at school. In our schools this means having lunch in our classroom; for others it might mean having lunch together in the school cafeteria.

Figure 12. Parents come and read to students

2. Decide on a time frame to invite family and other staff members to have lunch in the classroom.

3. Send invitations to families (see figure 13). Invitations may also be given to other staff in the school asking them to "come to lunch."

4. Have students greet guests as they arrive and invite them to come into the classroom and sit down for lunch. When guests leave, have students thank them for coming.

Dear Families,

The week of February 10 - 15 is "come to lunch" week. Bring your own lunch and brighten our day with your company.

Thank you,
Colleen

Figure 13. Invitation to "Come to Lunch"

IDEA #3 DROP IN AND DO

STEPS

1. Tell students that guests will be coming to the classroom to do an activity with them.

2. Set aside time during the class for guests to "drop in and do."

3. Develop a list of possible guests to invite, such as family members, adult friends, teachers, and support staff at the school. Send invitations to everyone on the list (see figure 14).

> Dear Families,
>
> You are invited to drop in and do an activity in our class on March 16th from 2:00 - 2:30 p.m. A student will welcome you when you arrive and explain what to do. We hope you can drop in.
>
> Thank you,
> Colleen

Figure 14. "Drop In and Do" invitation

4. Decide on the activity for "drop in and do." Choose something that students are familiar with such as playing a math game, reading a book, making a puzzle together, or working on a computer task. Give students time to practice the activity with a partner.

5. On the day of "drop in and do," give all students an independent task to work on until their guests arrive. Remind students to return to this task when their guests leave.

6. Have students welcome their guests as they arrive. We ask family members to work with their own son or daughter first and then, if they have time, to take part in an activity with at least one other student.

Introduction to Organization

Organize in ways that maximize learning.

■

Take time at the beginning to set up routines and procedures
with students; it saves time in the long run.

■

Organize in ways that allow all students to make independent
use of materials, spaces, and routines in the classroom.

■

Organization is more than having a neat and tidy
classroom. Organization is about creating a positive,
safe, and orderly environment.

■

The best way to organize is the way that
works best for you and your students.

In this chapter on organization, we offer practical ideas to
"spark" things up for you and your students during the year.
Activities include ways to:

- add novelty to transitions

- organize student presentations

- reorganize materials

- have partners provide learning support

- include new rituals to end the day

Your Turn:
making transitions novel and effective

DISCUSSION

The more we involve learners, the more they pay attention. We include students in the creation of new ideas to organize classroom transitions such as lining up, moving to a meeting area, or getting materials. Here are three easy and effective ways to add novelty to transitions.

IDEA #1 ON THE MOVE

STEPS

1. Make a list of cues currently used in class to let students know when it's their turn to move to a new activity (see figure 15).

2. Read the list to students and invite them to suggest new ideas. Add these to the list.

3. Give students cues from the chart or invite students to choose the cues that tell who can be "on the move."

It's your turn when you hear...

- the month of your birthday
- your name spelled aloud
- a type of shoe you have on
- a colour you are wearing

New Ideas

- your favourites
  (e.g., sport, colour, pet)
- how you got to school
- the colour of your hair
- the colour of your eyes
- you are wearing a watch
- you have velcro

Figure 15. Transitions "On the Move"

Idea #2 Who's on First?

Steps

1. Assign a number to each row or group of students. Make a chart to display a rotation system that shows the order in which each row or group will move to a new activity. We attach a clothes-peg to the chart to indicate which number will be the first to move (see figure 16).

2. Ask a student at the beginning of each day to move the clothes-peg to the next number. For an entire day, students seated in the designated row or group will move first. The second group to move will be the next number in the sequence, and so on.

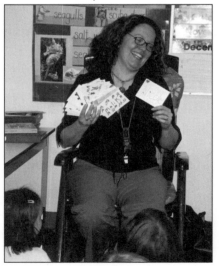

Figure 16. "Who's on First?"

3. Encourage students to look at the chart whenever there is a transition so they know "who's on first." We find that our students appreciate the fairness of this approach that gives everyone a turn to be first.

Idea #3 The Luck of the Draw

Steps

1. Make a deck of "class cards" by having each student print his/her name on a piece of paper (cardstock or an index card), and have each student draw a picture, or attach a photo of him/herself.

2. Use the cards any time you need to select a student or group of students.

3. Shuffle the deck, fan the cards out, and ask a student to pick one or more cards, depending on how many students are needed (see figure 17). Have the student read the name(s) out loud to indicate who is selected.

4. Ask the students to stand up when they hear their names called and listen for directions.

Figure 17. "Luck of the Draw"

Four Corners:
increasing opportunities to present to an audience

DISCUSSION

Learning improves when students have regular opportunities to present in front of an audience. One way to organize presentations is to have four students present simultaneously to four different groups of peers. We find our students are more comfortable presenting to a small group rather than to the whole class, and they are motivated by the attention and feedback they receive from their peers.

STEPS

1. Explain to the class that everyone is going to have an opportunity to be a presenter and an audience member in an activity called "four corners."

2. Draw a diagram on chart paper that shows the seating arrangement for "four corners" (see figure 18). Explain that the Xs on the diagram represent the presenters and the circles represent the audience.

3. Let students know that each presenter will have a "fair share" of audience members. We typically end up with four to six audience members in each corner.

4. Select six students to demonstrate "four corners." First, ask one student to be the presenter, have him/her find a short

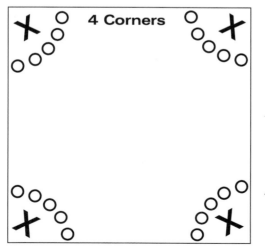

Figure 18. Four corners

piece to read, and ask this student to sit in a chair in one corner of the classroom. Next, ask five students to be audience members and have them sit on the floor in front of the presenter.

5. Continue the demonstration by asking the presenter to read for a few minutes to his/her audience. Stop the reader and ask volunteers from the audience to give specific compliments to their presenter.

6. Meet as a class on another day to clarify expectations for presenters and audience members. We ask students two questions: "What's important when you are a presenter?" "What's important when you are an audience member?" Record their responses on chart paper. We find our students need these lists to know exactly what is expected of them and how to give others specific compliments.

7. Give the students opportunities to practice "four corners." We set up a two-week schedule to accommodate the whole class. We start with a task that our students are very familiar with such as reading a poem, reading a favourite page from a book, or giving the daily news.

8. Take a few minutes after each "four corners" presentation to meet as a class and talk about what worked, what did not work, and what we could do to improve.

ADAPTATION

"Four corners" can be used with any kind of presentation including sharing personal writing, showing and talking about projects, sharing artwork, and reading jokes.

What's important when you are a presenter?

- present something you have practiced
- read so we can hear you
- speak clearly
- use expression
- stop at periods
- don't go too fast or too slow
- keep the book away from your face

What's important when you are a listener?

- sit quietly
- look at the presenter
- keep your hands and feet to yourself
- don't interrupt
- give compliments
- say "thank you"

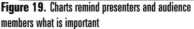
Figure 19. Charts remind presenters and audience members what is important

Check Mates:
providing support to a partner

> *"Scientists have long been aware of the effect that peer interaction has on cognition… others provide social safety, security, common identity, and meaning."*
>
> — Eric Jensen,
> *Learning Smarter:
> The New Science of Teaching*

DISCUSSION

Working with others supports learning and creates a source of positive energy in the classroom. We introduce "check mates" to help maintain and extend a learning climate that is cooperative, playful, active, and fun.

STEPS

1. Tell students they are each going to work with a partner, called a "check mate," who will help them at different times during the day.

2. Let students know that each person will have the same partner for one week at a time. Make a list of "check mates" and post it in the classroom. In the beginning, we select these partners for our students.

3. Give students simple tasks to do when they begin working with their "check mates" (see figure 20). For example, "Meet with your partner and check to see that you both have your names and the date on your papers. Return to your desks as soon as you are finished."

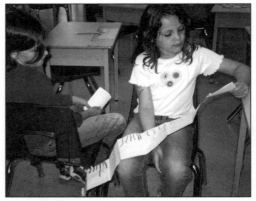

Figure 20. Check mates

4. Meet as a class after using "check mates" a few times. Clarify expectations by asking: "What's important when you work with your partner?" Make a list of the students' responses (see figure 21). Before they work with their partners again, we reread the list with students and use the phrases to tell them what they are doing well and what they need to improve.

5. Give students opportunities to work with "check mates" several times a day. Some of our favourite tasks include the following: reminding each other, reviewing key ideas, retelling steps, repeating directions, recalling specific information, and recognizing each other's efforts and successes.

6. Debrief at the end of the week by inviting volunteers to tell the class one way their partners helped them. Set up new partners for the following week.

What's important when you work with your partner?

- look at each other
- do the job the teacher gave us
- say "thank you"
- take turns
- be friendly
- talk quietly
- think about what they say
- be kind
- listen to your partner

Figure 21. What's Important for check mates

End of Day:
reflecting and connecting

DISCUSSION

Organize the end of the day in ways that help students leave with a good feeling about themselves and what they have accomplished. We have students clean up 5-10 minutes before class dismissal and use this time to end the day in relaxed and productive ways. We offer three of our favourite ideas.

IDEA #1 WHIP AROUND

STEPS

1. Have students sit in a circle after clean-up time is over.

2. Let students know that talking about learning helps them remember what they've learned.

3. Ask students a question, and have each student give a brief response or say "pass." We ask open-ended questions that have no right or wrong answers such as: "What is one thing you liked doing today?" "What do you like doing at recess?" "What do you want to have more time to do again tomorrow?" "What's one thing you learned about snakes today?"

IDEA #2 UPBEAT

STEPS

1. Let students know that it is important to leave at the end of the day feeling positive and "upbeat."

2. Give students time to clean up, organize all of their belongings, and then have them sit in their group or line up at the door.

3. Establish a goodbye ritual such as singing a song, listening to special music, doing an end-of-day chant or rap (see figure 22). Some of our favourite end-of-the-day songs are "Happy Trails to You," "Mickey Mouse," and "So Long, It's Been Good To Know You."

IDEA #3 LEAVING CONNECTED

STEPS

1. Let students know it is important to take a few seconds to connect with one another at the end of the day.

2. Have students suggest possible ways to say goodbye at the end of the day. Make a list of their responses (see figure 23).

3. Give students time to clean up, organize their belongings, and have them line up.

4. Ask students to choose one of the ways to say goodbye from the list they made earlier. Stand or sit so you are eye level with the students and have them walk past you, one at a time, to say goodbye in the way they chose (see figure 24).

End-of-Day Chant

One, two,
Clean up to do.
Three, four,
Line up at the door.
Five, six,
A partner you'll pick.
Seven, eight,
Tell something great.
Nine, ten,
See you again.

Black line master on p. 57

Figure 22. End-of-day chant

Ways to Say Goodbye

Let's look each other in the eye and say goodbye.

Your choice
- high 5
- hug
- hand shake
- smile
- wave
- thumbs up

Black line master on p. 58

Figure 23. Ways to say goodbye

Figure 24. Leaving connected, shaking hands

Taking Stock:
reorganizing materials
and reenergizing learners

"Once we have grown accustomed to an environment…it then becomes routine…and the brain gets less and less stimulation."

— Eric Jensen,
Completing the Puzzle

DISCUSSION

During the year, learning materials in the classroom can be lost, overlooked, or underused. One way to have students take a fresh look at what's available is to have them "take stock" and determine what needs to be replaced, recycled, repaired, or relabelled.

STEPS

1. Select one area of the classroom that needs to be reorganized, revitalized, and cleaned up. For example, we choose an area in the classroom that has many different materials, such as the math area.

2. Tell students they are going to "take stock" of the math materials in the classroom. Explain that "taking stock" means working in small groups to decide what needs to be replaced, recycled, repaired, or relabelled.

3. On a piece of chart paper, list all the math materials in the classroom. Ask for volunteers or assign areas where students will "take stock" (see figure 25).

Replace Recycle
Repair Relabel

- **games** Autumn Jenelle Kelly Jacob
- **math manipulatives** Chandra Sarif Cheryl Daniel Ami Asia
- **dice** Katrina Robin Rosalind Tony
- **unifix, multi-link blocks** Mateo Joseph Dyan Chantall
- **cards** Ravi Saxon Lexie Elizabeth
- **calculators, clocks** Lorne Andrea Wendall Kisha

Figure 25. Taking stock

4. Have a supply of paper and pens for students to make labels for new containers. Designate areas for recycling, and have paper towels available so students can wipe off materials.

5. Ask students to check in when they have finished taking stock. We sign our initials beside the task on the chart paper and take a photo of the reorganized area. This is displayed as a reminder of how the materials should be returned after they are used.

6. Have groups celebrate their reorganization by using the materials in new and unique ways. We encourage students to work with materials they have not used in a long time and to share their ideas with peers.

7. Meet as a class and invite students to talk about what they noticed when they were taking stock. Ask: "Did you find anything you forgot we had?" "Did you try out a different way to use any of the materials?" "Can you think of any new math materials you would like to have in the classroom?" "Are there any other areas in the classroom where we might need to take stock?"

ADAPTATION

Have students "take stock" in the classroom library to find out what books are available and organize, sort, label, and shelve books together. Regie Routman, in her book *Reading Essentials*, gives a detailed description of this idea.

Figure 26. Working with a check mate

Figure 27. Student shows class cards for "luck of the draw"

Figure 28. Check mates are retelling key information from a video

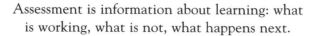

Assessment is information about learning: what
is working, what is not, what happens next.

■

Our first goal for assessment practices is to support
student learning, not simply measure it.

■

Descriptive feedback is what contributes most
dramatically to learning.

■

The more students are involved in their own assessment,
the more they learn.

■

Students are more likely to achieve goals they set
for themselves than ones set for them.

In this chapter on assessment, we offer practical ideas to
"spark" things up for you and your students during the year.
Activities include ways to:

■ involve students in setting criteria

■ teach peers how to give each other useful feedback

■ give learners specific, descriptive feedback

■ have students check their work

■ help students set realistic goals

Setting Criteria:
making the destination clear

DISCUSSION

Setting criteria with students is a powerful way to improve student behaviour and achievement. To set criteria with students we follow four steps: make a list, sort it into groups, post the chart paper, and add to and refine the list. When students are involved in the process of setting criteria they have a better understanding of what is expected of them and feel some ownership over their learning.

STEPS

1. Remind students what it means to set criteria and how it helps our learning. For example, say: "We are going to work together to make a list of what's important. When we do this, everyone will know exactly what they are supposed to be doing."

2. Start by developing criteria for something that students are familiar with, such as listening to someone read a story. On chart paper, print the question: "What's important when we are listening to someone read?" As students respond, record their exact words on the chart paper (see figure 29).

○ What's important ○ when we are listening to someone read?

- keep our hands and feet to ourselves as they read
- look at the reader
- look at the pictures
- sit on our bottoms
- listen carefully so you can answer questions
- sit still so others can see
- make pictures in your brain
- don't get in someone's space
- ask a question

Figure 29. Setting criteria

Adapted from *Knowing What Counts: Setting and Using Criteria*

When students run out of ideas, read the list to them and ask if they can think of any more. Then add important ideas that students have not yet mentioned.

3. Ask students to listen to a brief story. When you finish reading the story, reread the list created by the class. Ask the students to tell what they did that matched the ideas on the list. They might also think of new things to add to the list.

4. Ask students to watch and listen as you organize the list into groups of common ideas. We "think aloud" for students by saying: "I'm going to use a yellow pen to circle all the ideas about how we should sit. Now I'll use a red pen to circle all the ideas that we need to think about when we are listening." Continue organizing the ideas into groups by using different coloured pens to indicate each grouping.

5. Decide on a phrase that describes each group of ideas and record these phrases in a column on the left side of a piece of chart paper. These phrases are the criteria. In a column on the right hand side of the chart paper, list the students' and teacher's ideas opposite the appropriate phrases (see figure 30).

6. Post the list of criteria as a reminder of what listeners are expected to do. We offer feedback using words and phrases from the chart, and we ask students to give specific compliments to themselves and others.

7. Add to and refine the list of criteria. We sometimes find that we need to add ideas that have been missed. We can also include new and more complex ideas as students learn more and develop during the year.

○   ○

Listening to someone read

Criteria	Our Words
look at the reader	• look at the reader • look at the pictures
sit in a way so that everyone can listen and see	• sit on our bottoms • keep our hands and feet to ourselves as they read • don't get in someone's space • sit still so others can see
think about what you are hearing	• listen carefully so you can answer questions • make pictures in your brain • ask a question

Figure 30. Setting criteria

ADAPTATION

Make criteria more understandable for students by adding drawings, symbols, colours, or photos of students meeting the criteria. We also look for objects that represent each criterion. For example, to represent the criterion "look at the reader," we have a pair of plastic sunglasses.

Reading Train:
getting information from peers to support learning

DISCUSSION

Peers are important resources for each other. One way to tap into the power of peers is to introduce the idea of a "reading train." This activity provides regular opportunities for students to give and receive specific compliments.

Figure 31. Peers provide an audience and give information during "Reading Train"

STEPS

1. Make a sketch to show students the seating arrangement for the "reading train." Explain that half the class sits on Side 1 and reads something, and the other half sits on Side 2 and listens to their partner. We show our students a photograph (see figures 31 and 41).

2. Have six volunteers demonstrate the activity for the class. Ask three students to find a short piece of writing they want to read aloud. Have the three students form Side 1 of the train by sitting down, one student behind the other, in a designated area in the class. Ask the other three students to form Side 2 by sitting next to a Side 1 student.

3. Give a start signal and tell Side 1 students to begin reading to their Side 2 partners. After a few minutes, give a stop signal and ask Side 2 students to give one compliment to their reader. We use a train whistle to add fun and novelty to this activity. One whistle blow signals the start of the reading, and two whistle blows signal students to stop reading.

4. Continue demonstrating the activity by showing volunteers how to move "on the train." Show how Side 1 students move forward one place on the train. The person at the front of the line moves to the last place on the train. Side 2 students stay where they are. After the Side 1 students have moved, give the start signal for students to begin reading, from the beginning of their piece, to their new partners. Repeat the process one more time, and stop the demonstration after each student has worked with two or three partners.

5. Help students learn to give useful information to their partners by making a list of criteria together. We pose the question: "What's important when you read to someone?" Make a list of responses on chart paper (see figure 32).

6. Post the chart paper at the front of the "reading train." Remind listeners to use words and phrases on the list to give useful information to their partners.

7. Use the "reading train" with the whole class for any type of reading practice including jokes, poems, and nonfiction material. We try to make sure that we use "reading train" at least twice during the day so students have the opportunity to be both readers and listeners.

8. Meet as a group after using "reading train" and ask students: "What worked well during reading train?" "What do we need to improve?" "What changes can we make?"

> ## What's important when you read to someone?
>
> - pick something you can read pretty well
> - practice before you read so you sound good
> - pick interesting stuff
> - use a clear voice
> - make sure your partner can hear you
> - use expression
> - if you don't know a word you could ask your partner for help
> - remember to breathe
> - stop at periods
> - slow down for commas

Figure 32. Reading train

ADAPTATION

"Reading train" can be changed to a "writing train." In this case Side 1 students bring something they have written and read it to Side 2 students. The process can also work as a "math train," where Side 1 students bring math questions that they have completed, and explain exactly what steps they used to find the answer. An "art train" would mean students share and explain a piece of their artwork and Side 2 students give compliments.

Be Specific:
increasing descriptive feedback

"Feedback is considered to be the most important ingredient to enhance achievement (Marzano, 2000)."

— In Marilee Sprenger,
Becoming a "Wiz" at Brain-Based Teaching

DISCUSSION

To succeed, learners need specific information that describes what they are doing well and what they still need to work on. One of our challenges is to move away from using general statements such as "Great job!" and learn to be more specific and give clear information that students can use to improve. We offer two novel ways of giving descriptive feedback.

IDEA #1 WALKABOUT

STEPS

1. Explain the purpose of "walkabout" to students. "Your brain can do a better job when it gets information that tells it exactly what it is doing well and what it need to do to improve. When you start working, I am going to walk around and tell you what I notice about your work."

2. Select a task that students are familiar with. For example, we ask students to make a poster. We post a piece of chart paper showing criteria to remind students what is important (see figure 33). If we do not have criteria, we develop it with our students.

3. Read the criteria to the students before they begin working on their posters. Move through the classroom and make specific comments to individual students: "You have your name on your poster." "I see you are making the words big enough for people to read." "Look at all the bright colours! You are getting the attention of someone looking at your poster."

4. Reread the criteria to students who are having difficulty getting started. Ask them to identify one thing they plan to work on before you return on your next walkabout.

IDEA #2 CRITERIA PING-PONG

STEPS

1. Introduce "criteria ping-pong" using a task that students are familiar with. For example, we ask students to write a letter. We post a piece of chart paper showing criteria to remind students what is important (see figure 34). If we do not have criteria, we develop a list with our students before they start to work (see process page 28).

2. Explain the purpose of "criteria ping-pong" to students: "Your brain can do a better job when it gets useful information. I'm going to look at our list of criteria, walk around, and tell you what I notice you are doing. I might say: 'I notice you have the date written on your paper.' Then it is your turn to say something that you notice about your writing such as, 'I wrote, Dear Alice.' We go back and forth saying what we notice to one another, in the same way a ping-pong ball goes back and forth from player to player."

3. Read the criteria to the students and after they start writing, move around the classroom playing "criteria ping-pong" with as many students as you can.

4. Reread the criteria to students who are having difficulty getting started. Ask them to identify one thing for you to see when you return to play "criteria ping-pong."

ADAPTATION

Once students are familiar with receiving verbal feedback from their teacher during "walkabout" and "criteria ping-pong," they learn to take on the role of giving feedback to other students.

Making a poster

- use bright colors
- put your name on it
- use big letters so people can see your words
- don't use a lot of words
- make a picture that shows your idea
- make your picture big
- outline to make things stand out
- start in pencil then trace over the good parts
- spell it right

Figure 33. Students need to hear specific information during walkabout

What's important when you are writing a letter?

- start with Dear _____ ,
- put the date at the top
- tell at least three things to the person you are writing
- end with From, or Love, then your name underneath
- make pictures around the edge of the paper to make it fancy
- you can put a P.S.

Figure 34. Criteria ping-pong reminds students what they are doing well

Frame It:
involving learners in assessment

DISCUSSION

Many children think assessment is something done to them by an adult. One way to involve the students in their own assessment is to ask them to show or "frame" what they have done correctly and what they need to change. Students receive the immediate, specific feedback they need to be successful learners.

STEPS

1. Introduce "frame it" by using a task that students are familiar with. For example, we ask students to draw and write about their favourite part of a story. If we do not have criteria for the task, we work with students to develop a list of what is important before they begin to work (see figure 35).

2. Review the criteria by reading it aloud with the class before students start to work.

3. Give students time to work on the task. As they finish, show them how to place their work face up on the floor in the meeting area. At the end of the work period ask all students, including those who have not yet

Our Criteria

- make a picture that happened in the story (don't make it up)
- use details and make it colourful
- tell about it (in words) underneath your picture
- do your favourite part
- print in pencil
- put your name on it

Figure 35. Students need to know the criteria before they begin a task

finished, to bring their work and a pencil and come to the meeting area. Make sure all students place their work on the floor in front of them.

4. Demonstrate "frame it" to students. For example, say: "Most times when you finish your work, you bring it to me to have it checked. I'm going to show you a way to check your own work. First, watch me make a frame with my hands. Now you make a frame with your hands. Watch me 'frame' my name on the chart paper. Now use your hands to frame your name on your picture."

5. Watch what students do and coach them until they all understand how to "frame it." We find when students sit in a semicircle, we can quickly see who has met the criteria and who needs help (see figure 36). When we see students who have not yet met the criteria, such as putting their names on their papers, we ask them to put their names on their papers right then.

6. Continue reading different criteria aloud and ask students to "frame it" on their own work. We complete the activity by walking around the semi-circle and initialing or stamping each student's work to show them we've seen what they have done.

Figure 36. Students "frame" what they have done to meet the criteria

Goal Setting:
getting specific and realistic

"By facilitating students' attentional focus on personal goals and immediate feedback, we can actually help brains direct their attention by bringing these goals to a conscious level."

— Martha Kaufeldt,
Begin with the Brain

DISCUSSION

Children of all ages can learn to set their own goals. To help our students set specific and realistic goals, we focus on one skill or behaviour and ask students to choose a goal from a list we created together. Receiving support from partners and having celebrations add "spark" to keep students interested and involved.

STEPS

1. Talk to students about what goal setting is and how it can help them improve. For example, we say: "We are all good at some things and we all have things we need to work on. When you decide to work on something, this becomes your goal."

2. Decide on a class activity or time during the school day that needs improvement. We select something that students do on a regular basis, such as centre time, choice reading time (SSR, DEAR), clean-up time, or working with a partner.

How can we get better at using our centre time?

- have different people for partners
- don't just do one job all the time, try different things
- stay with one job for a while, don't keep changing jobs
- do your share of clean up
- if you make something, put your name on it, or put a name card with it
- let other kids join your group
- share
- get along
- don't yell
- use a quiet voice
- have good ideas
- use stuff in different ways

Figure 37. Class list of things to improve

Adapted from *Knowing What Counts: Self-Assessment and Goal Setting*

3. Work as a class, and make a list of things to improve. For example: "How can we get better at using our centre time?" Record the ideas on a piece of chart paper (see figure 37).

4. Read the list of ideas with students, and ask them to decide what they are already good at and what they might need to improve. Have each student select one thing he or she would like to work on.

5. Have students write or draw their goal on a card or piece of paper (see figure 38).

6. Provide time each day for students to meet briefly with a goal partner to talk about their goals. Have them ask each other: "What is your goal?" "How did you work on your goal today?" "What are you going to do next to get better?"

Figure 38. Student records a personal goal

7. Give students a short period of time to work on the goals they selected. We find that a week is often long enough for young children to stay focused on a specific goal.

8. Provide time for a brief celebration at the end of the week. We have goal partners stand side by side as we read one goal at a time from the list. When a student hears his/her goal, he/she turns and faces the goal partner. The students then show actions that best describe how well they met their goals (see figure 39).

Some of our favourite actions are as follows:

- Hold hands high, wave them back and forth, and sway the hips from side to side. This means: "Yes, I've made it!"

- Stretch arms out like an airplane with wings dipping from side to side. This means: "I'm getting there."

- Run on the spot with arms pumping. This means: "Still working on it!"

Figure 39. Students show their partners how well they met their goals

Figure 40. Goal partners talk about their goals

Figure 41. Students give useful feedback during reading train

Figure 42. Make criteria more understandable by adding photos of students and showing what is expected

Reliables are ideas that can be depended
on to keep students active and engaged.

■

Reliables are activities that work with a wide range of learners.

■

Reliables offer students choices to show what they know.

■

Reliables let students personalize their learning.

■

With reliables, students know what to anticipate,
and they can say: "Oh, we know how to do this!"

In this chapter on reliables, we offer practical ideas
to "spark" things up for you and your students
during the year. Activities include ways to:

- have students become survey leaders
- ask students for their opinions
- add more fun with poetry
- teach a routine for research
- include new stress busters

Class Surveys:
engaging learners and challenging thinking

DISCUSSION

Add variety to "spark up" the year. One reliable way to engage learners is to have them conduct class surveys and report the results. This activity is fun for learners and challenges them to think in new ways.

STEPS

1. Explain to students that a *survey* is when many people are asked the same question.

2. Demonstrate how to conduct a survey and how to report results. We "think aloud" so that students know exactly what they are expected to do. For example, we say: "First I need a survey question. One question I can ask is: 'Do you have a pet?' I think this is a good question because people can answer *yes* or *no*. Next, I will ask other people in our class and keep a record of the answers."

3. Continue to demonstrate and "think aloud," asking several students to answer the survey question. Show students how to record the results on a survey sheet by writing each student's initials under the "yes" or "no" column (see figure 44).

Figure 43. Two students conduct class surveys

4. Complete the demonstration by reporting the survey results to the class. We model how to use "sentence starters" to make reporting the results manageable for all students (see figure 45).

5. Develop a list of possible survey questions with students. Record all student suggestions on chart paper, without making any comments at this time. Read over each question with the whole class, and decide which questions can be answered with a simple *yes* or *no*, and which questions need to be changed or dropped.

6. Decide when the surveys will be conducted, who will be the survey leaders, and how many students will be conducting a survey at a time. We ask those who are interested in being survey leaders to write their names on slips of paper and put them in a container. One day a week (or anytime the classroom needs to be sparked up) we draw two names from the container. These two students select a question and complete a survey.

7. Have survey sheets available for students (see blackline master on p.60). We place the survey sheets on a clipboard, which adds novelty.

8. Have the class meet at a convenient time and ask survey leaders to report results. Ask each survey leader to end the session by asking: "What is one thing that the survey did not tell us?"

My Name: _____ Caren Cameron _____

My Question: _____ Do you have a pet? _____

Yes	No
A.D.	A.S.
S.C.	C.G.
P.T.	
M.O.	
D.G.	
S.S.	
M.N.	
C.C.	
C.P.	
K.G.	
Total 10	Total 2

Black line master on p. 59

Figure 44. Record the results on a survey sheet

My question was:
Do you have a pet?

I asked **12** people this question.

I found out that **10** people **have pets**.

I found out that **2** people **do not have pets**.

One thing the survey did not tell me was **what kinds of pets people have** .

Black line master on p. 60

Figure 45. Sentence starters

Your Opinion:
asking everyone to respond to a question

DISCUSSION

Most young children like to talk about themselves and give their opinions. We give students a chance to be heard by introducing an open-ended, reliable activity called "your opinion."

STEPS

1. Explain the purpose of "your opinion." For example: "There never seems to be enough time in our class to hear what everyone thinks about a topic. To give all of you a chance to let others know what's on your mind, and to find out what other people think, you are all going to write or draw your responses to a question at the same time. When you have finished, you will walk around the class and see what other people think."

2. Record the same open-ended question at the top of four to six pieces of

Your Opinion

returning from a field trip. Ask: **"What was the most interesting thing you saw today?"**

after watching a video. Ask: **"What two things did you learn about sharks?"**

after attending a school assembly. Ask: **"What part of the performance did you enjoy the most?"**

finding an item of interest in the news. Ask: **"What do you think should happen to the orphaned killer whale?"**

during a sports event. Ask: **"Who do you think will win the Stanley Cup? Why?"**

when responding to a specific problem at school. Ask: **"What can we do about the litter problem at school?"**

returning to school from holidays. Ask: **"What did you do on winter break?"**

Figure 46. Possible questions for "Your Opinion"

chart paper. Samples of questions we might ask are listed in figure 46. Place the sheets around the room; on tables, on the floor, or on the walls.

3. Divide the class into groups of four to six students, and assign each group to work on one sheet of chart paper.

4. Have all students read the question aloud. Give a signal for them to begin writing or drawing their responses on part of the chart paper (see figure 47).

5. Signal when time is up, and have students read or look at their own responses to see if they need to add anything. Have students move around the room so they can look at and read at least three other responses.

6. Post all pieces of chart paper together at the group meeting area. Have students come together, and ask volunteers to say something interesting or ask a question about someone else's response.

ADAPTATION

Each week, write a new question on one large sheet of paper. Invite students to find time during the week to write or draw their responses. Have students meet as a group at the end of the week to read and discuss other students' opinions.

Figure 47. Students record their opinions for others to see

Poetry Plus:
making time and finding an audience

"One of the most important life lessons that writing and reading poetry can teach our students is to help them reach into their well of feelings—their emotional lives…"

— Georgia Heard,
Awakening the Heart

DISCUSSION

Make time for poetry. We find using poems in a variety of ways keeps our students active and engaged. We offer three brief, playful ways for all students to select, read, and discuss poetry.

IDEA #1 PAUSE FOR A POEM

STEPS

1. Record "Pause for a Poem" on the class agenda, and explain to students that they are going to pause every day to listen to a poem.*

2. Demonstrate this activity by reading a short poem, and ask students to make comments or connections, or ask for a reread.

3. Invite interested students to sign up to read a poem. To help students succeed, we have them practice reading the poem to us (or to another adult) before they read it to the whole class.

4. Have a student read a poem to the class. Remind them to ask their peers for comments and connections at the end of the reading.

*Adapted from *For the Good of the Earth and the Sun*

IDEA #2 LUCKY LISTENERS

STEPS

1. Tell students they are going to read a poem to people outside the classroom.*

2. Give each student a copy of a poem that the class has read before.

3. Give students class time to practice reading the poem to a partner. Before they start, have them ask their partner: "Will you be my lucky listener?"

4. Have students find other "lucky listeners" in the school or at home. Have students ask their "lucky listeners" to sign their initials on the poem after they have listened to it.

5. Give students the chance to share their favourite stories about their lucky listeners.

*Adapted from Tim Rasinski, in conversation at California Reading Association, San Diego, CA, 2003.

IDEA #3 POETRY CHALLENGE

STEPS

1. Display a poster or an art print in the classroom at the beginning of the week.

2. Challenge students to work with a partner to find a poem that reflects the images in the poster or print.*

3. Choose a day at the end of the week to have each pair of students meet with another pair of students to share their poems (see figure 48). Have the students explain why their poem "fits" with the poster or print.

*Adapted from Nancy Polette, in conversation at the Early Literacy Conference, Portland, OR, 2001.

Figure 48. A student finds and reads a poem that "fits" with a poster

ADAPTATION

Use the idea of reading to "lucky listeners" with other writing genres. For example, plan a week for reading jokes, a week for reading facts from a nonfiction book, or have a week for looking at fairy tales.

Research Routines:
teaching an ongoing cycle

"Having choices in learning allows the student to begin with the positive emotional state associated with doing what he or she wants to do (McGeehan, 1999)."

— In Laura Erlauer, The Brain-Compatible Classroom

DISCUSSION

When students have choice, motivation increases. One way we offer choice is by teaching a research routine where students select a question, search for information, summarize the answer, and share with another person. This routine is a cycle that encourages students to work on questions that are important to them, at their own pace.

STEPS

1. Tell students that they are going to learn a research routine so they can select the questions that interest them the most.

2. Draw the four steps of the research routine so that it clearly shows the cycle (see figure 49).

3. Demonstrate the routine for students by working through each step of the

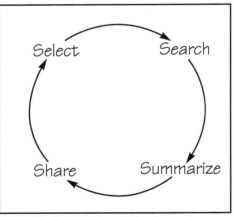

Figure 49. Four steps of a research cycle

cycle and filling out a research sheet (see figure 50). Show how to record a question in Box #1, list sources in Box #2, write a summary in Box #3, and in Box #4, share with a partner and have the partner sign his/her name.

4. Select a curriculum focus such as insects, and have the class work together to make a list of questions that they are interested in that relate to insects (see figure 51).

5. Give each student a file folder to hold their research, and make multiple copies of the research sheet for students (see black line master on p. 61).

6. Remind students that each time they finish the research cycle, they select a new question and start again.

7. Give students class time to work on their research. When they have searched and still cannot find an answer, they select a new question and start over. Remind students that the next time they work on their research, they begin where they previously left off. We reassure students that looking at the pictures in books, even if they can't read the words, is a good way to find information.

8. Meet as a group at the end of each research time and discuss: "What worked well today?" "What didn't work well today?" "What can we do next time to make it work better?"

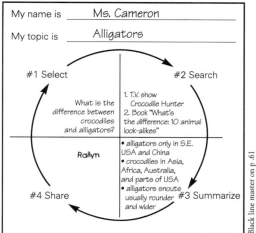

Figure 50. Four steps of a research cycle

Black line master on p. 61

Figure 51. Research questions

Stress Busters:
increasing interactions and reenergizing learners

"… studies indicate that physical activity aids the learning brain… (Kesslak, et al. 1998)."

— In Eric Jensen,
Learning With the Body in Mind

DISCUSSION

Add a few minutes of movement each day to reenergize learners so they can be more productive. Three of our favourite "stress busters" are described below.

IDEA #1 WALK AND TALK

STEPS

1. Tell students that getting up, moving around, and talking with others helps them take care of stress so they can be better learners.

2. Teach a new "stress buster" called, "walk and talk." Ask a pair of student volunteers

Figure 52. Students take time to walk and talk when the music starts

to follow these directions (see figure 52): "Find a partner and, when the music starts, walk around the room together. Talk to each other and return to your place when the music ends."

3. Give simple prompts to get students talking: "Tell a favourite part of…" "Tell a fact you recall about…" "Tell two things you already know about…"

4. Give students frequent opportunities to "walk and talk" until it is a reliable class routine. Emphasize the importance of returning to work as soon as the music stops.

Idea #2: Look in the Mirror

Steps

1. Have students sit or stand face to face with a partner.

2. Give a rule to determine who is the first leader. For example, the person who has the longest hair is the leader.

3. Ask the leader to make slow movements with his/her hands and arms.

4. Tell the follower to copy the movements of his/her partner carefully, so that it appears as though he/she is looking in a mirror.

Figure 53. Students try to show matching signs in "Cooperative Rock-Paper-Scissors"

5. Ask the partners to change roles.

6. Add music after students have practiced this activity a few times. We use songs that have slow tempos such as, "Somewhere Over the Rainbow," "What a Wonderful World," "Memories Are Made of This."

Idea #3 Cooperative Rock-Paper-Scissors

Steps

1. Show students the three different signs to indicate *Rock-Paper-Scissors*. A clenched fist signifies the rock, an open hand with the palm facing down indicates paper, and extending the index and middle fingers, but hiding the other fingers, is the action for scissors.

2. Have students stand back-to-back with their partners. Tell them that the goal is to have both students show the same hand signal. As students stand back-to-back they "put their heads together" and try to guess what signal their partner will show.

3. Count: "1,2,3" out loud. On the count of three, ask students to turn, face their partners, and show their rock, paper, or scissors hand signals. When students "match" signals they congratulate each other and try to repeat their success. When students do not "match" signals, they try again.

4. Repeat the process two or three times, just for fun, and then have students resume working with renewed energy.

Appendix A
professional development

USING THIS BOOK WITH ADULT LEARNERS

The ideas in this book can be used to support professional development activities in different settings; for example, educator's book clubs; team and department meetings and staff meetings; and in-service and pre-service workshops.

Consider the following possibilities:

BRAIN BITS

This idea works well as a way to introduce the book at a staff meeting (where only two or three books might be available).

1. Make a copy of Brain Bits black line master (page 62) for each participant.

2. Organize the participants into small groups (three or four per group), and have each member in the group do the following:

   (a) Choose a "brain bit."

   (b) Read aloud the quotation to the others in the group.

   (c) Discuss how he/she can relate the "brain bit" to his/her students and experiences in the classroom.

   (d) Invite group members to make comments or ask questions.

3. Have the groups continue until each person in the group has had a turn.

4. Bring all the groups together, show them copies of Voices of Experience, and invite a couple of volunteers to read the books and try some of the ideas with their students.

5. At the next staff meeting, ask the volunteers to discuss what ideas they tried and what they learned.

JIGSAW

Jigsaw is a quick way to introduce the book to the participants. This idea works well at staff meetings or pre-service teacher seminars (when there are large numbers of participants).

1. Divide participants into groups of four. Assign a different section of the book (Relationships, Organization, Assessment, Reliables) to each person in the group.

2. Ask each person to read his/her assigned section and to be prepared to summarize and retell a favourite activity.

3. Each person, in the group of four, takes a turn to talk about his/her section.

4. Invite participants to select one idea that they will try out with their students. Ask each person to come to the next meeting with student samples and stories to share.

BOOK CLUB

This idea works when at least two people are interested in the book.

1. Invite colleagues to form a book club (two or more people make a club).

2. Agree on a time and place for the first meeting.

3. At the meeting, decide how to work with the book. A couple of suggestions: (a) each member reads a different section of the book and selects one activity to try with students, or (b) the group comes to an agreement on one section of the book to read and one idea to have everyone try out before the book club meets again.

4. At the end of the meeting, set a time to get together again. Agree to bring back student samples and stories about what worked, what did not work, and what adaptations were made.

5. Invite participants to record their next steps on a planning sheet (see page 63).

INDEPENDENT STUDY

This idea works well for teachers who choose to work on their own – especially those who are new to the profession and those who are working at a new grade level.

1. Read the book to get an overall sense of its contents (20 ideas for a 20-minute read).

2. Select one or two ideas to try out with students.

3. Use the record sheet to keep track of the idea you have tried, how well it worked, and what idea to try next (see Recording Sheet, page 64).

TAKE ACTION

This idea works well at meetings and workshops.

1. Invite adult learners to try out activities for themselves during staff meetings and workshops. Here are some possibilities:

■ "Setting Criteria" (page 28)

Have staff or other working groups develop criteria or expectations for working together. For example: What is important for staff meetings to be productive?

■ "Stress Busters" (page 48)

Choose one or two Stress Busters, and have participants try out these ideas during meetings or workshops.

- "Check Mates" (page 20)

  Ask adult learners to find a "check mate" at the beginning of a workshop or meeting. Stop two or three times and ask "check mates" to meet to share and compare their thoughts.

- "Four Corners" (page 18)

  Save time at a staff meeting or a workshop by using "four corners." Have participants share information such as professional reading, highlights from a workshop, or favourite classroom activities.

- "Your Opinion" (page 42)

  Use "your opinion" to have participants give their personal views. Everyone gets to see what others are thinking and it leads to active discussion.

Appendix B
black line masters

Dear Families,

Our class has been learning about _____.
We will use the last hour on _____
to have a party to celebrate our learning. Sharing
food adds to a celebration. Your child has volunteered to bring _____. If this works
for you please send it on the morning of the party. If
not, please send something else, or let me know if we
need to make other arrangements.

Thank you,

Figure 3. (page 5)

Dear Families,

Your child _____ has volunteered to bring his/her collection of _____ to present to the class on _____ .

To help everyone be successful we suggest children follow these sentence starters for their presentations:

My collection is...

Three things I want you to notice are...

One thing that might surprise you is...

Does anyone have any questions?

Please ask me some questions about my collection of...

There will be a space set aside in the classroom for collections to be displayed.

Thank you,

P.S. Please do not send anything that is "too precious to lose."

Figure 9. (page 11)

End-of-Day Chant

One, two,

Clean up to do.

Three, four,

Line up at the door.

Five, six,

A partner you'll pick.

Seven, eight,

Tell something great.

Nine, ten,

See you again.

Figure 22. (page 23)

Ways to Say Goodbye

Let's look each other in the eye and say goodbye.

Your choice

- high 5
- hug
- hand shake
- smile
- wave
- thumbs up

Figure 23. (page 23)

Survey Sheet

My Name: _____

My Question: _____

_____

Yes	No

Total _____   Total _____

Figure 44. (page 41)

My question was:

_____

I asked _____ people this question.

I found out that _____ people have _____.

I found out that _____ people do not have _____.

One thing the survey did not tell me was

_____

_____ .

Figure 45. (page 41)

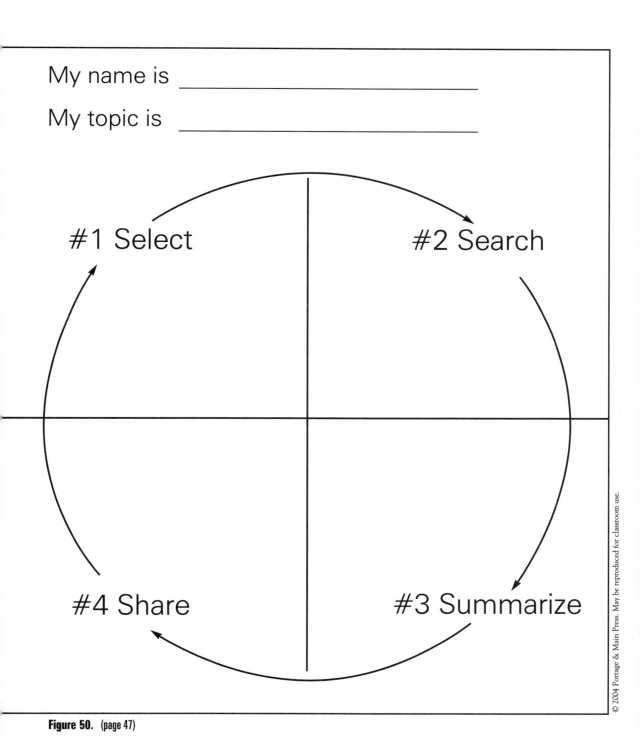

My name is _____

My topic is _____

#1 Select

#2 Search

#4 Share

#3 Summarize

Figure 50. (page 47)

1. "Modeling love of learning and creating a classroom environment where rituals and celebrations are dealt with are foundations for emotional well being."
   - Colleen Politano, Joy Paquin, *Brain-Based Learning With Class*

2. "The saying, 'the best way to learn something is to teach it,' contains more than a little truth."
   - Patricia Wolfe, *Brain Matters*

3. "When students work hard…they are anxious to have friends and family view their efforts and help celebrate their work."
   - Martha Kaufeldt, *Begin With the Brain*

4. "Scientists have long been aware of the effect that peer interaction has on cognition…others provide social safety, security, common identity, and meaning."
   - Eric Jensen, *Learning Smarter: The New Science of Teaching*

5. "Once we have grown accustomed to an environment…it then becomes routine…and the brain gets less and less stimulation."
   - Eric Jensen, *Completing the Puzzle*

6. "Feedback is considered to be the most important ingredient to enhance achievement (Marzano, 2000)."
   - In Marilee B. Sprenger, *Becoming a "Wiz" at Brain-Based Teaching*

7. "By facilitating students' attentional focus on personal goals and immediate feedback, we can actually help brains direct their attention by bringing these goals to a conscious level."
   - Martha Kaufeldt, *Begin with the Brain*

8. "One of the most important life lessons that writing and reading poetry can teach our students is to help them reach into their well of feelings—their emotional lives..."
   - Georgia Heard, *Awakening the Heart*

9. "Having choices in learning allows the student to begin with the positive emotional state associated with doing what he or she wants to do (McGeehan, 1999)."
   - In Laura Erlauer, *The Brain-Compatible Classroom*

10. "…studies indicate that physical activity aids…the learning brain…(Kesslak, et al. 1998).
    - In Eric Jensen, *Learning With the Body in Mind*

Planning Sheet **Name:** _____

The section I'm focusing on is _____

_____

The idea I'm going to try is _____

_____

_____

Subject/topic/assignment I'm using it for is _____

_____

Time frame: by _____

_____

Comments:

What worked: _____

_____

_____

What didn't work: _____

_____

_____

Adaptations made: _____

_____

_____

Planning Sheet

Recording Sheet	**Name:** _____	
Contents	**Ideas Tried**	**Comments**
RELATIONSHIPS 　Introduction to Relationships 　Learning Parties 　Kid-directed Centres 　Trading Spaces 　Collections 　Family Connections		
ORGANIZATION 　Introduction to Organization 　Your Turn 　Four Corners 　Check Mates 　End of day 　Taking Stock		
ASSESSMENT 　Introduction to Assessment 　Setting Criteria 　Reading Train 　Be Specific 　Frame It 　Goal Setting		
RELIABLES 　Introduction to Reliables 　Class Surveys 　Your Opinion 　Poetry Plus 　Research Routines 　Stress Busters		

Recording Sheet

Bibliography

Erlauer, Laura. *The Brain-Compatible Classroom: Using What We Know About Learning to Improve Teaching.* Alexandria, VA: Association for Supervision and Curriculum Developement (ASCD), 2003.

Given, Barbara. *Teaching to the Brain's Natural Learning Systems.* Alexandria, VA: Association for Supervision and Curriculum Developement (ASCD), 2002.

Gregory, Kathleen, Caren Camreron, Anne Davies. *Knowing What Counts: Setting and Using Criteria.* Merville, BC: Connections Publishing, 1997.

———. *Knowing What Counts: Self-Assessment and Goal-Setting.* Merville, BC: Connections Publishing, 2000.

Heard, Georgia. *Awakening the Heart: Exploring Poetry in Elementary and Middle School.* Portsmouth, NH: Heinemann, 1999.

Heard, Georgia. *For the Good of the Earth and the Sun: Teaching Poetry.* Portsmouth, NH: Heinemann, 1989.

Jensen, Eric. *Completing the Puzzle.* Del Mar, CA. Turning Point Publishing, 1996.

Jensen, Eric. *Learning with the Body in Mind: The Scientific Basis for Energizers, Movement, Play, Games, and Physical Education.* San Diego, CA: The Brain Store, 2000.

Jensen, Eric, Michael Dabney. *Learning Smarter: The New Science of Teaching.* San Diego, CA: The Brain Store, 2000.

Jocelyn, Marthe. *Hannah's Collections.* Toronto, ON: Tundra Books, 2000.

Kaufeldt, Martha. *Begin with the Brain: Orchestrating the Learner-Centered Classroom.* Tucson, AZ: Zephyr Press, 1999.

Polette, Nancy. In conversation at the Early Literacy Conference, Portland, OR, 2001.

_____. *Learning Smarter: The New Science of Teaching.* San Diego, CA: The Brain Store, 2000.

Politano, Colleen, et al. *Voices of Experience: Practical Ideas to Start Up the Year.* Winnipeg, MB: Portage and Main Press, MB, 2004.

Politano, Colleen, Joy Paquin. *Brain-Based Learning With Class.* Winnipeg, MB: Portage and Main Press, MB, 2000.

Routman, Regie. *Reading Essentials: The Specifics You Need to Teach Reading Well.* Portsmouth, NH: Heinemann, 2003.

Sprenger, Marilee. *Becoming a "Wiz" at Brain-Based Teaching: How to Make Every Year Your Best Year.* Thousand Oaks, CA: Corwin Press, 2002.

Wolfe, Patricia. *Brain Matters:Translating Research Into Classroom Practice.* Alexandra, VA. Association for Supervision and Curriculum Development (ASCD), 2001.

Workshops

The authors are available to do workshops on the Voices of Experience series of books. If you enjoyed this book, you'll love their workshops!

Here's what participants are saying:

"Brilliant. Thank you for giving me such wonderful ideas to take back to my class."

"The ideas are easy, inexpensive, and require little preparation."

"Great energy. Wonderful ideas that can be used immediately!"

"Many of your ideas will show up in my class this week. Thanks, too, for the chuckles."

"Thanks, I had fun. I learned a lot and my kids will benefit right away."

"Your ideas help me do the best for my students and still have a life for myself."

For more information, please contact Portage & Main Press at 1-800-667-9673.